OFFICE DIRTY TRICKS

By Hunter S. Fulghum
Illustrations by Barrie Maguire

00 01 02 03 10 9 8 7 6 5 4 3 2 1

ISBN: 0-7407-0986-0

Office Dirty Tricks is produced by becker&mayer!, Kirkland, Washington.
www.beckermayer.com

Edited by Jennifer Doyle • Design by Victor Mingovits • Production by Barbara Galvani

OFFICE DIRTY TRICKS

50 Ways to Sabotage Your Coworkers and Bluff Your Way to the Top

By Hunter S. Fulghum
Illustrations by Barrie Maguire

Andrews McMeel Publishing

Kansas City

HARD WORK IS ITS OWN REWARD... NOT!

"Work smarter, not harder."

Business managers love to toss out nuggets of wisdom such as this. But somehow they forget to mention that not only do you have to try and work out for yourself what this nonsense means, you have to do so while sitting in a small, metal cube with inadequate ventilation while a computer monitor fries your brain. Like deciphering the riddle of the Sphinx, if only you had the solution, you'd be in Fat City—in this case the big chair in the corner office, with stock options, a company car, and six weeks paid vacation every year.

Bad news, folks. If you're interested in climbing to the top of the corporate ladder, you've got stiff competition. Every one of your coworkers heard the same words of wisdom at the last staff meeting, and they're all busy trying to "work smarter" just like you. If any of them *do* figure it out, you're toast. What you need is an edge—a guiding light to point you in the right direction. Fortunately, you've come to the right place: this book. It's filled with the tricks, rules, and helpful hints to help you work *sneakier,* not harder.

When all else fails, remember this: Don't get mad, get promoted!

INHABITANTS OF
THE OFFICE JUNGLE

Who Are These Animals, Anyway?

General Sherman once said, "War is hell." Obviously he never worked in an office; otherwise he would have added, "But office life *really* sucks!" He also would have advised us to apply to the office environment one of the most basic principles of warfare: "Know your enemy." With that in mind, here is a quick guide to identifying the most common inhabitants of the office (both coworkers and bosses), with useful information on their habits and behaviors.

The Brown-Nosed Kneeler

Also known as the "Nodding Yes Man" and closely related to the "Chapped-Lipped Butt Kisser," this coworker can be found in close proximity to the boss—any boss. He likes to preface statements with "Well, management thinks..." and nod frequently and enthusiastically during staff meetings, even when the discussion is about the stocking of feminine hygiene products in the ladies' room.

To identify the Brown-Nosed Kneeler in your office, listen for a sucking sound.

The Temporally Challenged Summer Migrant

Businesses get around child labor laws and unfair working conditions by making use of "interns." Interns are paid less than anyone else in the company and given the justification that running copies and fetching coffee for permanent staff is "real-world work experience."

To identify the Summer Migrant in your office, look for an expression similar to that of a deer caught in the headlights of a Mack truck. Another dead giveaway is the stack of important documents caught in the feed rollers of the copier.

The Cubicle-Nesting Time Killer

This coworker has been there since dinosaurs walked the earth, and is about as productive. He's perfected the trick of sleeping with paper in one hand, pen poised in the other, and has excellent radar—he immediately starts writing whenever anyone gets within ten feet of his cubicle. Check his pulse and respiration regularly.

To identify the Cubicle-Nesting Time Killer in your office, ask around. When you mention him by name, most people will respond with "Who?"

The Silicon-Based Techno-Warrior

Warning! This coworker is an exceedingly dangerous life-form capable of entering into search-and-destroy missions on your or anyone else's computer. He hacks IRS and Soviet Defense Ministry mainframes during lunch breaks. Treat with caution and respect—and whenever possible, suck up (see Helpful Hint #4).

To identify the Silicon-Based Techno-Warrior in your office, look for a ponytail and pierced body parts—and that "funky" smell.

The Pink-Fringed Bleeding Heart

Always in charge of human resources or employee morale, this boss believes there are no bad employees—just "misunderstood" ones. Poor performance is the result of a tough home life or a bad workplace environment. If you need some time off, she'll send you to counseling on the company's nickel. Tell her you're into a new type of therapy called "Kansan Internal Neo-Kinetic Indecentification" (KINKI)—and yes, Mistress Paradise *is* a preferred provider under the company's health plan.

To identify the Pink-Fringed Bleeding Heart in your office, figure out who chairs the company picnic committee.

The Flip-Flopping Chameleon

Also known as "Flavor of the Week," this boss—when he isn't devouring books, periodicals, and self-help instructional tapes that tell him how to succeed—is in the business section of Barnes & Noble looking for new materials. Two ways to deal with him: Recommend all the books you've "read" just to keep him in a constant state of catch-up, or make up a new business theory that involves him sending you home early.

To identify the Flip-Flopping Chameleon in your office, look for books by Tom Peters and posters with motivational messages.

Patton

This boss believes that a loud voice and an unshakable belief in his desire to prevail will overcome all obstacles—no matter what. He loves no one, but hunts the Brown-Nosed Kneeler for sport.

The Patton in your office is the one who yells the most. If he's your direct supervisor, may God have mercy on your soul.

OFFICE DIRTY TRICKS

The Squirting Calculator

Using the squirting calculator that comes with this book yourself won't win you any friends. But it's a darned good tool for sabotaging somebody else. Find some numbers dweeb in the office who's always pulling out his calculator in front of the boss or an important client to "run the numbers." Fill the phony calculator with water and substitute it for his real one right before an important meeting. Make sure the boss or client sits within your victim's line of fire. Filling the calculator with permanent ink is also an option. (Black and blue are both nice colors, but so are mauve or pink.)

Blame It on Someone Else

When dealing with an unhappy client, remember one basic rule: It's always someone else's fault.

When a problem occurs on a critical account and the customer calls in a rage, sigh loudly, *tsk* a couple of times, then admit to the caller, "We've been having that problem lately. [Insert coworker's name here] hasn't been the same since the accident. A head injury. Sadly, he doesn't even remember it, much less what he's supposed to do today." Never mind that it was you who caused the problem. Just make sure you solve it—and get the credit.

It's in the Mail...

Use office mail to your advantage—whether to torpedo someone else or to raise your stock in the boss's eyes. Since most mail is opened (and therefore probably read if it looks even remotely interesting) by administrative staff (who are generally the best sources of gossip in the company), you can spread all kinds of interesting tidbits of information for the minuscule cost of a first-class stamp. Order a subscription to the scuzziest skin magazine you can find, in the name of your most hated coworker. Pay for it in cash or with a money order and have it delivered to the office. You can also send this person the results of his testing for sexually transmitted diseases, the balance due on his Hair Club for Men account, a bill for his impotency treatment, or a notice to appear in court for public indecency.

Technology Is Your Ally

Crack an enemy
coworker's voice-mail
code. This is easier
than you think; most
people use their birth
date, last four digits of
their Social Security
number, and other
personal numbers that
you should easily be
able to find out. Change
his outgoing message to
something like "Hello.
You've reached the

voice-mail box of [coworker's name]. I'm just too busy to talk to you right now. Leave a number. I might get back to you." Sometimes it takes weeks before people change their outgoing message.

When new hires start, volunteer to show them the ropes for their first few days—little things like how to fill out a time sheet, program their voice mail, and set up a network password. Be sure to advise them that short, simple, easy-to-remember passwords are best, and changing their password is an invitation to forget it.

Pucker Up

The point of your career is to get ahead, no matter what the cost. By gum, that's the American way! So remember who hands out the perks, bennies, and

raises. Don't be ashamed to be a toadie or suck-up—just don't let your coworkers see you doing it.

Hate and Discontent I

Start removing certain items from the office, either stuff that belongs to other people (such as favorite coffee cups) or necessary office supplies (like all the pens in the supply cabinet). Soon everyone will begin to get suspicious and cantankerous. At the next staff meeting, stand up and denounce the mystery thief. Demand that he stop at once and return the stolen goods.

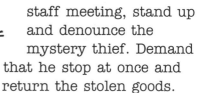

The next day, secretly return the pilfered items (except for the really good stuff). A week later, ask for a raise.

Hate and Discontent II

The office refrigerator is a godsend to the practitioner of Office Dirty Tricks. Not only is it good grazing grounds for when you forget to pack a lunch, it represents a prime opportunity to practice a little psychological warfare. Make a habit of stealing the really good contents from your coworkers' lunch bags and consuming them quickly, disposing of all remnants. After a few days, people will get annoyed and begin to search for the culprit. When the tension reaches this level, keep stealing the good stuff, but plant the tidbits you don't eat in the wastebasket of a coworker you don't like. When he is "caught," comment to others in the office on his gluttony and total disregard for his fellow workers.

The All-Nighter

Needed: three used coffee cups, fifteen wrappers (candy, doughnuts, potato chips, etc.), 451 pieces of crumpled-up paper, and eight broken pencils; one-day growth of beard (especially impressive on a woman).

Stay late at work, diligently pounding away at your computer. It doesn't matter what you're really doing—playing a video game or surfing the Web—so long as you make it appear that you are completely focused on a project. Wait until the last person has left the office, then go home. Sleep in the clothes you left the office in. Get up early the next morning and don't shave, shower, brush your teeth, or change your clothes. Arrive at the office early in the morning, before anyone else. Scatter your candy wrappers, empty cups, and other debris around, then finish your game of Doom or downloading files from Mistress Paradise's home page while you wait for the rest of the office to show up. As your boss enters the room, wearily lift your head and announce, "Finished." Let your head hit the desk in a final spasm of exhaustion. He'll be so impressed with your diligence that he won't even ask what it was you finished. And you'll probably get sent home early for a good rest, too!

Solving Problems that Don't Exist: Y2K+1

Remember the Y2K scare of 1999? "Oh no, the Millennium Bug is going to get us! Oh NOOOO!" What the "Millennium Bug" really did was keep a bunch of people working on a problem that turned out not to be one. Sounds like a pretty sweet deal. Mention to your boss that the experts are now talking—quietly, of course, so as not to create a panic—about the real problem: Y2K+1. Offer to research this problem on behalf of the company. Get yourself a good-sized staff (old college cronies are a good place to start) and a private suite of offices to work in—all on the company's nickel, of course. At the end of the year, announce complete success, as evidenced by the lack of system crashes. But what about next year? And the one after that?

Happy Birthday to You

Everyone tries to suck up to the boss at one time or another. The boss's birthday is a prime time for this, when the staff gets him a cake, a card, and some useless knickknack for his desk like one of those plaques that say "World's Greatest Boss." On the sly, spread the word that your boss really doesn't like having his birthday recognized—it reminds him of a bad childhood memory, like when his great-aunt Ola had a heart attack while baking him a cake on his twelfth birthday. Quietly invite the boss someplace really nice for his birthday and commiserate with him about his "self-absorbed, ungrateful employees." Don't worry about the cost of the meal—just charge it to a client account.

It's the Little Annoying Things that Truly Make Life Worthwhile

In this day and age, we have come to depend on technology to get things done. And when things don't go right, we immediately blame a technological glitch. This means a coworker can be busy debugging his computer, trying to discover the source of the lockup, for hours or even days before noticing that someone has removed the ball from his mouse. Or un-plugged his keyboard. Or faded the contrast on his monitor to black.

The Old Switcheroo

All cubicles look alike. Over a weekend, relocate a coworker's belongings to an empty cubicle, lock, stock, and family portrait. Arrange everything just as it was in the old cubicle, down to the trash in the trash can and the coffee stains on the desktop. When your coworker comes in on Monday, see how long it takes him to find his cubicle. Be sure to act as though his cubicle has always been next to Carol's. If you're convincing enough, the dupe and the rest of the office will believe this is the way the seating arrangement has always been. Extra credit for the really cruel: The following weekend, after the stooge has settled into his new space, move all his stuff back to the old one. This may be enough to cause a complete mental meltdown.

Quality Is Job One

For any company to operate properly, it requires a rigorous quality-control program. And usually the people who run these programs are either petty tyrants or incapable of doing anything else. Either way, it's an opportunity to have a little fun. Volunteer for the job and make it clear to your coworkers that you expect nothing but per-fection. Demand random samples of their work and

stalk off to "review it" with an evil scowl on your face, muttering obscenities.

Ignore the work for a few days, then return it to your coworkers with memos attached, telling them that the details (spelling, punctuation, grammar, and facts) are "adequate," but the tone and intent are completely wrong. Demand rewrites. Repeat the process until you get bored with torturing everyone. In the meantime, as your coworkers struggle to make you happy, they're getting behind on their other work—a fact that, as the quality control person, you feel compelled to mention to the boss.

Alternately, you can always use this position to extort favors from the coworkers you are harassing. Baked goods, small gifts, money, and the use of their cars on weekends are all fair game.

An Eye for an Eye

You don't need to be loved, but you should always be feared. If people think you're capable of serious professional retribution, they'll never cross you. If they think you're capable of personal retribution, including keying the paint not only on their car, but of every car in their neighborhood, they'll leave offerings at your office door.

Photocopying Body Parts

The old standby of photocopying body parts can go one better. After hours, photocopy a few intimate body parts. Then, in a handwriting style as dissimilar to yours as you can manage, address the copies to the boss and sign them "with love" from a coworker you can't stand. Leave the copies in the document tray of the machine.

Casual Tuesday

Send official-looking but utterly bogus interoffice memos to your least favorite coworkers, advising them that "Tuesday is dress-down day. By company policy, employees are encouraged to wear Bermuda shorts, Hawaiian shirts, and flip-flops." Be sure that the day you choose also happens to be the day of the first meeting with a very formal client.

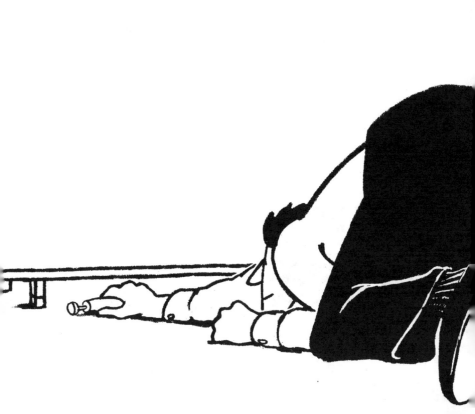

The War on Drugs

If a coworker deserves a particularly inventive method of torture, remind him that the best way to beat a drug test is to eat poppy seed muffins three meals a day for a week beforehand. While he's being confronted with drug test results that scream heroin use, scatter oregano and cigarette papers under his desk. A used syringe and a length of rubber hose are a nice touch, too.

Pass the Buck

The buck stops here. As it happens, "here" is not your in-basket. Accept the power, but never the responsibility. If you have a hard time with this concept, just reflect on the Reagan and Clinton presidencies.

It's All in the Presentation

Since more and more people are using presentation software, most of their materials are kept on computer. Do a little snooping and find a coworker's files, then use a scanner to digitize and substitute your own artwork and graphics into his presentation materials the night before he delivers them to a major client. Children's drawings and Viagra ads are both good options. Also be sure to change the spelling of the client's name.

Time- and Date-Stamp Everything

Work during regular hours, but reset your computer's clock to eight hours ahead. That way, documents and e-mail developed at 3:00 in the afternoon will look like they were written at 11:00 at night.

A Room of One's Own

Is your work space too small? Consider the fact that conference rooms have lots of room to stretch out. Sign up on the schedule for the room you like best, claiming it indefinitely under "Special Projects." Start moving in files and documents, spreading them across the table. You can hide out in there for weeks, even take naps. The boss may look in on you periodically—but if you perfect your "I'm-so-busy-I-can't-fit-it-all-into-my-office-and-I-need-some-peace-and-quiet" look, you might even score a bigger office out of the deal.

Crossing the Language Barrier

If your company works with foreign firms, offer to teach your coworkers useful expressions that will ease their relationships with these clients. For example:

French: Pourquoi ne cherchez-vous pas un vrai boulot?
Translation: *Why don't you get a real job?*

Italian: Tuo padre e un pollo.
Translation: *Your father is a chicken.*

Spanish: Estoy avergonzado conocerle.
Translation: *I am ashamed to know you.*

German: Ich wünsche zum fondle Ihre Hinterteile.
Translation: *I wish to fondle your buttocks.*

Japanese: Instruct your coworkers that *Tonkatsu* is a very high honorific in Japanese, better than *san* when attached to the end of a name. Thus, they should address Mr. Muramoto as "Muramoto-Tonkatsu."
Translation: Mr. Muramoto is fried pork cutlet.

When in Rome...

They say travel broadens one's outlook and is a great opportunity to learn. When your least favorite coworker gets an opportunity to travel to other parts of the country or (better still) overseas, offer him the benefit of your experience as a seasoned traveler by suggesting a few useful tips on traditional customs and dress. For example:

Southern United States: Advise your coworker to take along sunscreen as a gift, explaining that he should offer it to his Southern business contacts as a lotion to combat "redneck."

California: During meals, order beef—the rarer the better—or preferably veal.

Europe: Advise your coworker to let Western Europeans

know we really enjoyed protecting them from communism all those years when they weren't capable of looking after themselves. Extra credit: Tell your coworker that when taking business associates out for dinner, the French have a particular love of McDonald's.

Asia: Share this little-known fact with your coworker: the traditional Asian bow also involves a head-butt.

The former Soviet Union and Eastern Bloc countries:
Tell your coworker to be sure to let them know that we
don't think poorly of them even though we won.

Latin America: If your coworker is traveling to Central
or South America, remind him that a traditional hostess
gift is powdered sugar. But he should remove the
wrapper, pack it in plastic wrap, and wrap it in brown
paper so as to have it more closely resemble a gift.

It Might Be Terminal

Whenever you catch a cold or the flu, make sure you come into the office, at least initially. Play up the coughing, wheezing, sneezing, and achiness until the boss sends you home. He'll remember your "dedication to the job." Until he does send you home, be sure to shake coworkers' hands and use their coffee mugs when they aren't looking. With a little effort, you can infect the entire department and make yourself look even more dedicated when they don't show up for work.

The Customer Is Always Right

Get some good quality, blank stationery at an office supply store. Compose yourself a glowing recommendation from a fictitious client raving about the incredible quality of your work, your attention to detail, your willingness to go above and beyond the call of duty, and particularly the fact that you (and only you) are the reason the letter writer brings his business to your firm.

Address the letter to your boss, and mail it from across town—or (better still) from out of town if you have a distant friend who owes you a favor. Make the letter short and lacking in detail so it can't be traced to anyone, particularly you—just so the letter makes it clear how much your company should value your services. Sign it with a scrawled signature no one can read.

Join the Club

If you haven't already, take up golf. Golf is the glue that binds the brotherhood and sisterhood of the business world. Never mind that it's an expensive, difficult sport that involves chasing little white balls around an over-maintained patch of grass. Yeah, the pants look stupid. So?

Reach Out and Touch Someone

These days, you have to be connected to get ahead. One of your coworkers is bound to have clients, or contacts within the company, who could be very helpful to you.

Access the coworker's voice-mail box (see Dirty Trick #4) and leave a message that he is "away on a nine-week cruise and completely unavailable." Direct the caller to dial your extension for immediate assistance. After you politely and enthusiastically help them out, the client will probably forget all about the other guy.

Always Overestimate What You'll Need

• Double your time estimate for any task. Any time you don't use can be spent playing computer games or cruising the Internet for live webcam sites—or you can finish "early" and develop a reputation as a miracle worker.

• When developing budgets, triple the amount of money you really need—they'll just cut it in half, anyway.

• When asked how much manpower you need, the answer is simple: more than you've got now.

Flying the Friendly Skies

When you have to travel with people from your office, offer to make the travel arrangements. Alas, you and your coworker got booked on separate flights! It's a shame your coworker got seated in a middle seat at the very back of the plane next to a screaming child...on every one of the five legs between Seattle and Oakland. When you finally meet up with your haggard coworker at the hotel, you can swap tales about the horrible experience—never mind that you were enjoying chicken cordon bleu and complimentary champagne up in first class on a direct flight.

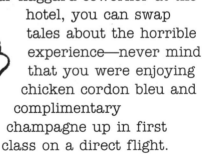

The Real Power Base

Remember where the power really lies: with the administrative staff. When they aren't happy, ain't *noooobody* happy. If you have a hard time sucking up to admin, remember this: Who else knows that the two-week "vacation" a coworker took was really a stint at rehab? Who else can look the other way while approving expense accounts—without asking why you were watching "Bare-Naked Coed Volleyball" on hotel pay-per-view? 'Nuf said.

Crushing the Spirit

Enthusiastic new coworkers have the potential to raise morale in the office and actually make a difference. As such, they are an extreme threat to you and must be crushed as quickly as possible. The most effective way of accomplishing this is to engage them in mind-numbingly dull tasks that take up huge amounts of time and are utterly ignored by management. As the new employee begins to sour, encourage him to make suggestions for change— especially ones that are utterly impractical and impossible. In no time at all, the new guy will develop an attitude that can't help but make yours look stellar.

The Power of the Laptop

Companies invest in laptop computers in order to gain greater productivity from their employees. After all, you can take a portable computer home and work there, too. The good news is: Laptops work both ways. A laptop can be a prime way of giving

the impression that you are working extra hours when really you're just lounging on the sofa sucking back a couple of frosty ones.

Dial into your company's computer network at odd hours of the night and on weekends, and randomly download and upload huge files. Hang off on sending e-mails—especially critical ones needed to make decisions the next morning—until late in the evening, to give hated coworkers no chance to think, act, or respond. Take your laptop on vacation and dial into the office once a day like you're working. By the official Office Dirty Trick rules, a few minutes of work done while on vacation are worth an hour of pay on the time card, minimum.

For the Good of the Team

Every so often, the company will decide to do something to improve "team spirit." This usually means a consultant has gotten to a manager and convinced him that carting his staff off to some godforsaken wilderness to climb ropes and eat mud for a few days will do wonders for the team.

It sounds dreadful, but all is not lost. When the course instructor asks for a volunteer to demonstrate trust by falling backward from a dangerous height into the arms of a coworker, volunteer—to do the catching.

As your most despised coworker takes his turn and begins to fall toward your waiting arms, let a look of shock come over your face as you spy a "rattlesnake" in the brush at the feet of another member of the team (preferably another coworker you don't like). Leap forward and plow into him (remembering to plant your shoulder in his kidney), knocking him clear of danger and saving the day.

As you help the coworker you failed to catch off the ground, explain to him that it was a matter of weighing certain death against serious injury. And be sure to send flowers.

Paging Bill Smith...

There is nothing more annoying than getting stuck in a dull-ass meeting. When one looms imminent, have your significant other call the office posing as your biggest client, with a dilemma only you can solve. Have the "client" insist you be found, no matter where you are.

Tossing a grenade like this into the office machinery will get your coworkers in a frenzy—searching you out, paging you, checking the stalls in the rest room—until they find you in the middle of the meeting. Look mildly annoyed at them for interrupting and taking you away from the stimulating discussion about the pros and cons of the competition's electric dog polisher. Promise to come back as soon as you can, remembering that this is twenty-five minutes after the meeting is scheduled to conclude.

Since all boring meetings run over by thirty minutes, this way you'll only have to endure another five.

When you get back to your office, close the door, put your feet up, and have a nice long chat with your savior. Optionally, you may choose to have phone sex.

LANs, WANs, and Power Outages

There is an axiom in business: Never go any longer without saving a computer file you are working on than the span of time you are willing to spend re-creating your work. Most people need to learn this lesson the hard way. Repeatedly.

Know where the power panel is in your office? How long would it take you to locate and flip the circuit breaker serving the cubicles of a few hated coworkers? Can you time it to, say, a crunch production period? Of course you can.

Or, using your hacked access codes to coworkers' accounts, spend an evening or two logged in under their names and passwords. Cruise a few XXX Web sites, download a few adult pictures, maybe convert them to screen-savers on coworkers' computers or e-mail them to the office prude with a personal note like: "Love to see you in THIS!"

The Disappearing Document

No matter how dependent we get on computers, we will always love wood products. The smooth feel of bond paper. The sense of security we feel when we tuck important documents into file folders. Just knowing the document is there is a good feeling.

So how do you suppose your coworker will feel when the critical paperwork he has so carefully preserved has vanished? Where could it have gone? Why, into some other folder, one that has absolutely nothing to do with anything even closely related to the project at hand (such as one of the folders in your office).

The best time to make the switch is right before the contents of the file folders are needed for an essential meeting. As your coworker frantically trashes his office looking for the documents, the boss will become more and more unhappy. At the eleventh hour, magically "come across" the file, explaining that you found it in the men's room tucked inside the sports page.

Denial Is Your Friend

No matter how onerous or tactless you act, never apologize or admit you were wrong. Donald Trump didn't when he screwed the pooch financially, so why should you?

The Elixir of Life

People who have trouble getting their hearts going in the morning are of little threat or consequence. Try switching the supply of regular coffee with decaf and vice versa. Sit back and watch all the caffeine junkies falling asleep in meetings, and all the really quiet people bouncing off the walls. Stick to tea until someone figures it out.

A Room with a View

Pick your least favorite coworker, the uglier and more offensive the better. Start sending him anonymous notes, just coy little suggestions at first about how much you like him, then moving on to more "serious" suggestions. Follow up with flowers, small gifts, and a few mysterious calls to his home (hanging up as soon as he answers).

Finally, rent a hotel room near the office and get three keys. Send one to your victim, along with a note that says, "I WANT YOU NOW!" and instructions to be in the hotel room, naked, at noon. Take the second key and send it to the most feared manager in the company, along with a note suggesting that he show up at the same room at 12:10 for a little surprise.

Give the third key, a Polaroid camera, and a $20 bill to the bellhop, with instructions to pay a visit to the room at 12:11.

Why Don't You Call Me Sometime?

You probably have a coworker who just can't live without his pager or cell phone. This is the guy who also insists on leaving his electronic toys on during meetings. Clearly he gets some thrill from the constant ringing. And God forbid he has one of those pagers that plays a

FOR A
REALLY
GREAT
TIME
CALL
253-881-1211

little musical ditty. How many times do you have to listen to the first three bars of the "Macarena" before you feel an urge to strangle the guy with his own small intestine?

Negative reinforcement is said to help you stop smoking. Apply the same principle here.

Get the guy's cell phone or pager number and visit the men's room of the sleaziest country-western bar in town, someplace frequented by cowboy wannabes on the make for a fine bit of filly. Write his cell or pager number on the wall of every stall and above every urinal in two-inch-high red letters, along with the promise of a "really good time." You can embellish the details of what you think is a good time on your own.

Passing the Plate

It's a regular-as-clockwork deal around the office: Someone wanders around with a brown envelope and a card of some kind (birthday, condolence, congratulations, etc.), collecting cash for a gift and well wishes for some coworker.

Collections of this nature can be characterized as nothing short of a rich opportunity.

As a civic-minded individual, you

should volunteer to take on this responsibility—particularly when the gift is for a high-level manager. People will undoubtedly ask you how much they should give. To find an answer for them, figure out the amount of money required to buy the gift you have in mind, divide it by the number of people donating to the pot, and then double the amount. Don't you need to be compensated for *your* time and trouble?

The Real Power Base II

Remember the Silicon-Based Techno-Warrior? Guess who's in charge of the office computer network? He thinks he's God, and he may be right—so treat him accordingly just to be safe.

Thinking Inside the Box

Every company has some means for employees to provide suggestions for improving the workplace. Most employees hesitate to contribute comments for fear of retribution. Give them good reason to do so.

Steal some of those "From the Desk of..." pads from a coworker you can't stand. Write down a few unpleasant personal observations about the company, management, and especially the manager who empties the suggestion box.

The Right Man for the Job

There are a lot of unpleasant tasks around an office that somebody has to do. Most people dodge these. You shouldn't. These chores are rife with opportunity.

For instance, as the Office Move Coordinator, you are in the position of trading the best cubicle assignments for favors, bribes, or cash. With a little imagination, anything is possible.

How about office supplies? Someone's got to be in charge of stocking office supplies. If it's someone else, you get your pick of all the weak crap that everyone else gets—the cheap desk, the slow computer, etc. But if you're in charge? Can you say "hand-carved, mahogany desk"? "Solid silver fountain pens"? "A Cray super computer"?

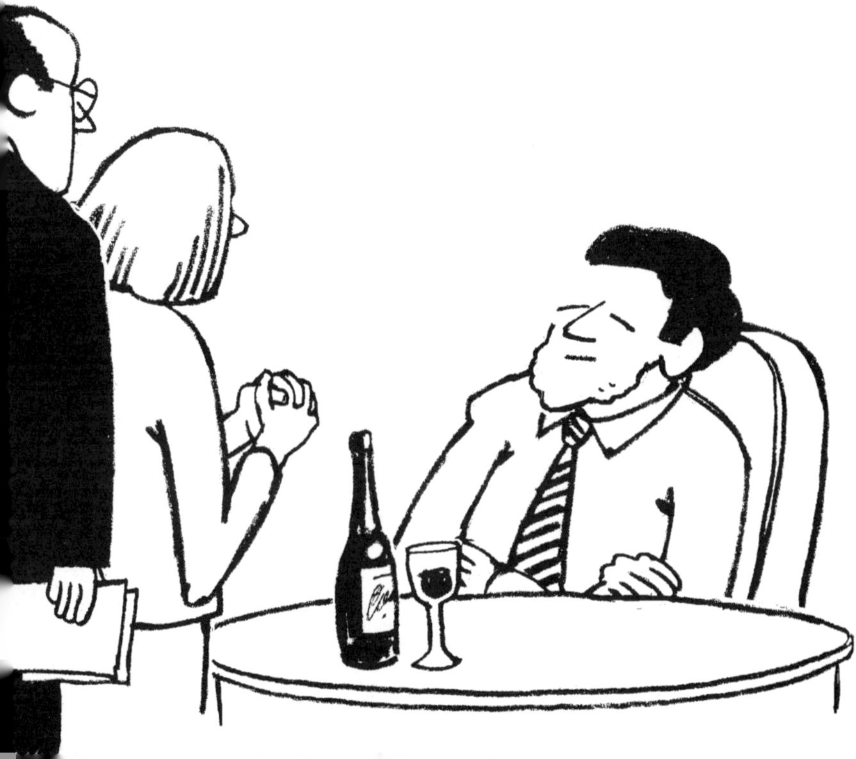

OFFICE DIRTY TRICKS
FOR THE PROMOTED

Keeping Down the Unwashed Masses

If you succeed in your goal of rising in power and prestige within the company, congratulations! You have now made the first great step up. As a supervisor or manager, there's a whole new set of tips, tricks, and guidelines to consider. Your goal is twofold: Not only must you look out for the best interest of your department, but you must also squelch any employee uprisings that threaten to topple you from power.

Raiders of the Best Parts...

As a leader, it is up to you to attract the best people to your department and to help them achieve peak performance (and to take the credit yourself). The easiest way to do this is to raid the best people from other departments. Use every

opportunity to assess the employees of fellow managers. Pay close attention to who gets praised during staff meetings. Peruse employee personnel files on weekends. When you've confirmed that an employee is a prime target, start planting seeds. Casually mention to another member of the staff (preferably the office gossip) that the employee you want is a candidate for a layoff in an impending "downsize"—and that's a tragedy, because you'd take him in a heartbeat. When the news reaches the employee and you get wind of his unhappiness, pull him aside for a little "off-line" chat. Make it clear that you're there for him. And so is that vacant cubicle in your department.

Be wary! Your competition may be setting you up for a Staff Infection (see Office Dirty Trick #37).

Staff Infections

Just as you want to
attract the best and
brightest employees
to your department,
you want to dump
the worst—
preferably on
your
competition.
Speak
glowingly of
your worst
people, place
great documen-
tation of their

successes (make up whatever you have to) in their personnel files, and above all, when another manager (let's call him Charlie) is shorthanded and needs help, offer to transfer the losers, one at a time or en masse, to his department. Immediately fill the vacancy in your department with a winner, to prevent Charlie from returning the reject.

When the employee crashes and burns outside your sphere of influence and you get challenged for it, look stunned, apologize profusely, and mumble something about how the workload must have gotten to him. Then go tell the boss that you're concerned about Charlie's interpersonal and employee-management skills, since he's letting good people go.

Beg Forgiveness, Not Permission

So you want to take the company car out four-wheeling on some back road in Montana or upgrade your airline ticket to first class? If you ask, the answer will be no. If you don't ask and you don't get caught, who cares? And if you do get caught, fall back on the best defense ever invented in business: "I was just thinking about the best interests of the firm." Remember, your happiness *is* in the best interests of the firm.

A Hostile Work Environment

Invariably as a manager, you will get an employee who threatens your position of power. Hassling him into submission will take time you won't feel like taking away from golf. Instead, create what is called a "hostile work environment." One of the best ways to do this is to give him the wrong access code for the office security system, so when he walks into the building, he can't override the alarm. Ask him to work on a Saturday. Then call office security and report that a known child molester/drug lord has been trying to break into the building on weekends.

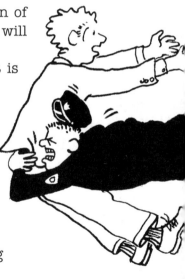

Giving Back to the Community

Every company feels the need to at least *appear* to give something back to the community. This can include blood drives, cleaning up parks, or collecting food and toys for the less fortunate. Somewhere in the management ranks above you is a boss who supports these charitable activities with an almost fanatical attitude.

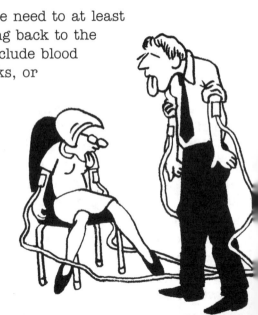

If you are to make the right impression with

this individual, it is absolutely essential that you support these efforts.

God forbid you should do any work yourself, or let the activity cost you precious time or staff productivity. So always schedule these events on weekends or after regular hours. It's implied that they are *volunteer,* so why should you have to pay for it?

This trick also lends itself to dealing out a little abuse to employees you really can't stand. During the blood drive, for example, tell your least favorite staffers that management has hinted that anyone who donates TWO pints during this year's drive will be smiled upon by the company. With luck, these people will go for it and as a result experience a higher incidence of illness and absence, in which case you can write them up for failure to show up for work.

Sorry, It's Company Policy

There is nothing like the company policy manual to bring out the weasel in someone. As a manager, you have a prime opportunity to issue edicts that may as well have been cut into stone tablets and handed to Moses. Policies are the LAW, and failure to conform can result in being cast into the fiery pit, so to speak.

If you have an employee or two that you really need to beat down into the ground, try issuing a few policy manual updates to them. Make it a casual event—drop a few into their in-baskets when they're not around. Don't make any public acknowledgment of the new requirements.

As for the policies, let your creative side go to town. Here are a few seeds to get you started:

"Effective immediately, all employees will park no closer than one (1) mile from the office, to encourage better cardiovascular health through exercise."

"Effective immediately, all employees are required to greet senior staff as 'Captain, my captain.'"

"In accordance with the company's green initiative, all paper products shall not be discarded or recycled until fully used. Employees shall use both sides of any paper, including envelopes, flyers, facial tissue, or toilet paper, prior to disposal."

About the Author

At the tender age of eighteen, Hunter S. Fulghum was stolen from his parents by a roving band of corporate raiders and sold into indentured servitude with a heartless, faceless corporation. The most important lesson he has learned is that the best means of survival in the corporate food chain is to be at the top. Never one to shy from an ambitious goal, he hopes to complete his first hostile corporate takeover before he turns forty. He has never been convicted of insider trading, influence peddling, embezzlement, fraud, blackmail, or any other white-collar crime that has resulted in him being a "guest" of the state in a country club prison. Yet.